singers
of the blues

Victoria Spivey, blues singer and composer. Born in Houston, Texas, she worked with many of the great blues singers of the 1920's. She starred in the film *Hallelujah* (1929) and during the 1930's led a hot jazz band in the Middle West. In 1961 she made a comeback. She toured Europe with the American Folk-Blues Festival in 1963, and added to her long list of recordings, which date back to 1926.

A Pull Ahead Book

singers
of the blues

Frank Surge

Lerner Publications Company   •   Minneapolis, Minnesota

784.0922
Surge

ACKNOWLEDGEMENTS: The illustrations are reproduced through the courtesy of: pp. 2, 11, 47, Victoria Spivey, Len Kunstadt Photos; p. 5, Chess Records, Don S. Bronstein Photo; pp. 6, 9, 14, 28, Independent Picture Service; pp. 13, 16, 18, 22, 24, 33, 41, Duncan P. Schiedt; pp. 27, 37, Dr. Edmond Souchon; p. 45, MGM Verve Records; pp. 48, 50, 53, 54, 56, 59, 60, 63, Raeburn Flerlage, Delmark Collection.

"Black, Brown and White" by Big Bill Broonzy
© Cassell and Company Ltd., London
from BIG BILL BLUES: William Broonzy's Story
as told to Yannick Bruyhoghe
© 1955, 1964 Oak Publications, Inc., New York
Used by Permission

"Back Water Blues" by Bessie Smith
© 1927, 1955 Empress Music, Inc.
Used by Permission
"Strange Fruit" by Billie Holiday
© Edward B. Marks Music Corporation
Used by Permission

The Library of Congress cataloged the
original printing of this title as follows:

Surge, Frank.
    Singers of the blues. Minneapolis, Lerner Publications Co.
[1969]

    64 p. illus., ports. 21 cm. (A Pull Ahead Book)

    Brief biographies of seventeen singers and musicians who
helped develop the blues style and became legendary performers
during their lifetime.

    1. Singers, American—Juvenile literature. 2. Jazz musicians
—Juvenile literature. [1. Negro musicians. 2. Jazz musicians.
3. Singers, American] I. Title.

ML3930.A2S9   784'.0922 [920]   68-30570/MN
ISBN 0-8225-0453-7   MARC

                                                         A C

Muddy Waters

contents

Deckhands on a Mississippi riverboat. Their spirituals and work songs were forerunners of the blues.

What Are The Blues?

Somewhere on a city street, at the center of a small group of people, stands a shabby-looking old man. In his hands he holds a guitar. His fingers seem to fly about the strings without effort, first fast and wild, then slow and quiet. Then the old man begins to sing. He sings about lost love or hard work or homesickness, about a dead friend or an auto accident or a neighbor woman. He makes up the song as he goes along. Sometimes he stops during the song and talks to his small audience, explaining something about the song or perhaps telling a joke that has just come to him. Often he repeats a line of the song for emphasis or to give himself time to create the next line. Even when he repeats, he makes the second time sound a little different from the first.

His voice has a rough, husky quality. He has his own sound, and he is proud that it is different from anyone else's sound. It is what he created out of himself, a part of him that no one can take away. He "plays" his voice as if it is a musical instrument. He slides it up and down and slurs his notes together without a clear break between them. He deliberately sings some notes just a little flat, giving them a *blue* sound. The sliding and slurring and blue notes give the song a sad, haunting quality, but the old man sings with a gusto that adds a touch of joy to the sadness. It's as if he is saying "Life can be rough, but I'm not going to let it beat me down." He is singing the blues.

Where did these blues come from? Where did an un-educated old man learn to make such music? The answer goes back hundreds of years to the time of the slave ships from Africa. At that time the proud and beautiful black people, who had a complex culture centered in music and dance, were mistaken for ignorant savages, put into chains, and taken to America to do the white man's work. They learned the white man's language and took up the white man's religion. They were completely cut off from a home-land they could never hope to see again. They were a people without a past. But they did have one way of hang-ing on to their African identity, and that was their way of making music. This was the heritage that they passed on to their children.

Often a slave, working in the cotton field, would raise his head and shout out his misery in the form of a chant. This *field holler* would ease his troubled spirit and make his work more bearable for him. Sometimes groups of slaves working together would sing as they worked. A leader would call out a line of the song, and the group would respond with a refrain. The leader would make up new lines, and the group would repeat the same refrain after each line. These *work songs* were not only an enter-tainment for the slaves as they labored. They served the purpose of helping the men work together, in rhythm, instead of working against each other.

The blues emerged from the field holler and work song of the cotton field.

When the Protestant missionaries tried to teach the slaves their religion, they brought along their hymn books and taught the hymns to the slaves. But the slaves didn't follow the books. They sang the hymns in their African style and sometimes even danced in their churches. In this way they created *spirituals* and *ring shouts*.

The Americans in the South, unlike the French and Spanish in the West Indies, did not allow their slaves to play the drums. Thus the slaves in the South lost some of the complicated rhythms that their brothers in the West Indies continued to use. But even without the drums they preserved some of the rhythms by clapping and stomping them, and finally they and their descendants began to play these rhythms on the guitar.

Field hollers, work songs, spirituals, ring shouts, and guitar rhythms — take something of each, mix it all together, and you have the beginning of the country blues. Later, as the freed Negroes moved into the cities, their music was played on brass and woodwind instruments. Singers began to take their subject matter from city life. When they sang with bands and made records they did less improvising and developed a set form for their songs. Or sometimes they started with a set form, and then with the accompanying band they would improvise within that form. These various forms and styles have been called urban blues, classic blues, and jazz blues.

This book is a tribute to the blues men and blues women who sang, and continue to sing, straight from the heart, creating music that endures.

Little Brother Montgomery, Victoria Spivey, Lonnie Johnson, and Sonny Greer, after a recording session, 1965.

Ma Rainey

Gertrude Malissa Nix Pridgett, who was to become Ma Rainey, Mother of the Blues, was born April 26, 1886, in Columbus, Georgia. She first performed in public as a child in a talent show called "The Bunch of Blackberries." At 14 she attracted the attention of Will Rainey, who was in Columbus with his traveling show, the Rabbit Foot Minstrels. Within a year they were married. Gertrude became the show's main attraction. For 35 years she toured the South's Negro vaudeville circuit, performing in theatres and barns and living in a house trailer.

For her act she drew songs and ideas from many sources: minstrel, vaudeville, burlesque, circus and carnival songs, folk ballads, and country blues. She was always close to the people and the people's music. She listened to the traveling blues singers, the jug bands, and the fiddlers. She took the country blues songs, shaped them with the things she had learned, transformed them with her own artistry, and produced a kind of song and style that came to be called "classic blues."

Audiences loved Ma Rainey. She was not a beautiful woman, but she had a warm personality and a pixie face that had an appeal of its own. On stage she wore a beaded band around her uncombed hair. She wore earrings made of gold coins and a chain of gold pieces around her neck. And she usually held a huge fan made of ostrich feathers.

Ma Rainey and her Georgia Band

Louis Armstrong

In 1923 she began to record her songs, and over a period of six years her records made her famous throughout the country. On some of these records she is accompanied by a young cornetist named Louis Armstrong. Some of the songs she recorded were "Levee Camp Moan" and "Moonshine Blues." "See See Rider," sung and recorded by Ma Rainey and many other older Negro singers, was revived in the 1960's by young rock-and-roll groups, who picked up much of their material from the early blues pioneers.

After her mother's death in 1933, Ma Rainey retired from show business and settled in Rome, Georgia. She lived there until her death on December 22, 1939.

Bessie Smith

Ma Rainey earned the title "Mother of the Blues." Bessie Smith, who learned from Ma and took up where she left off, also earned herself a title, "Empress of the Blues." It was an accurate title, for no other classic blues singer could equal Bessie Smith during her good years.

Bessie was born April 15, 1898, in Chattanooga, Tennessee. Life was hard for Bessie, her brother, and her three sisters. Raised in poverty, they had to work and scrape for every mouthful of food and stitch of clothing. In grade school Bessie liked to act in school plays, and even then her singing voice was attracting attention. When she was nine she performed at the Ivory Theatre in Chattanooga. When she got her first week's salary of $8, she sneaked off and bought herself a pair of roller skates. She got a spanking from her mother for buying roller skates when the family needed food.

In 1910 the Rabbit Foot Minstrels came to Chattanooga. Ma Rainey heard Bessie and decided to take her into the act. For a while she was billed as a child singer, but soon her voice and personality were too strong and she began to sing as an adult. Bessie and Ma were opposites in appearance. Bessie wore simple dresses. She kept her hair swept back. Her only jewelry was one strand of beads around her neck. She was a tall, good-looking woman.

Bessie Smith, 1925

After a few years Bessie left the Rainey show and began to work by herself in saloons and dance halls around the South.

By 1919 she was popular throughout the South and had a show of her own, "Liberty Belles," in an Atlanta theatre. By now she was already moving into the role of Empress, and insisted on being called Miss Bessie. On February 16, 1923, she made her first record, "Down Hearted Blues" and "Gulf Coast Blues." This record sky-rocketed her to the top. On April 7, 1923, she married Jack Gee, a Philadelphia policeman. Eventually, when she wasn't traveling, she made her home in Philadelphia.

The next five years were Bessie's best years. Her voice and style made corny songs sound good. She had that certain ability that distinguishes the real blues singers from the fakes; the ability to give the happy songs a touch of sadness and the bitter songs a touch of spirit. Bessie didn't sing in the old country blues style. She was an urban singer. She preferred to sing with trained musicians like trombonist Charlie Green and pianist James P. Johnson rather than with the country guitarists. This made her popular with blacks who had left the South and moved to northern cities, because they wanted to forget the old days.

By 1925 fame and fortune had come to the poor girl from Chattanooga. Bessie was very generous with her money, and many so-called friends took advantage of her generosity. In 1926 she began to write her own songs.

Bessie Smith in the film *St. Louis Blues,* 1929

"Gin House Blues" gave a hint of the dark road ahead. "Back Water Blues," a description of floods on the Mississippi, was a work of art. "Empty Bed Blues" was one of her most popular songs. "Me and My Gin" told a true story, for Bessie was becoming a heavy drinker. The public taste in music was changing, and she was losing her popularity. She struck back with one of her best songs, "Nobody Knows You When You're Down and Out," which expressed her bitterness toward the leeches who were turning away when she needed them.

In 1930 she and Jack separated. Her records failed. Her voice cracked. But she went down singing. In 1933 she made another hit record, "Gimme a Pigfoot (And a Bottle of Beer)." This refers to the old beer joint practice of serving free pickled pigsfeet with the beer. Her last record, also made in 1933, was "I'm Down in the Dumps." For the next three years the Empress of the Blues sold gum and candy in theater aisles. She accepted "mammy" roles in cabarets. She sang dirty songs in cheap saloons.

Then things began to look up. In February 1936 she appeared in a blues and jazz concert. Then came a six-week engagement in a show. A recording session was planned. A film offer came from Hollywood.

In September 1937 Bessie was being driven South to join a show in Memphis. The car in which she was a passenger crashed into a parked truck, and Bessie was seriously injured. She died in the Negro ward of G. T. Thomas Hospital in Clarksdale, Mississippi. Some say that she bled to death while the injured whites were treated first.

Bessie Smith was buried in Darby, Pennsylvania. Her grave was unmarked until 1970, when the late blues-rock singer Janis Joplin and a Philadelphia nurse, Juanita Green, shared the cost of erecting a headstone. The inscription on the headstone read:

THE GREATEST BLUES SINGER IN THE WORLD

WILL NEVER STOP SINGING

BESSIE SMITH

1895-1937

Back Water Blues

When it rains five days and the skies turn dark at night
When it rains five days and the skies turn dark at night
Then trouble's takin' place in the lowlands at night.

I woke up this mornin', can't even get out of my door
I woke up this mornin', can't even get out of my door
There's enough trouble to make a poor girl wonder where she wanna go.

Then they rowed a little boat about five miles 'cross a pond
Then they rowed a little boat about five miles 'cross a pond
I packed all my clothes, throwed 'em in and they rowed me along.

When it thunders and lightnin' and the wind begin to blow
When it thunders and lightnin' and the wind begin to blow
There's thousands of people ain't got no place to go.

Then I went and stood upon some high old lonesome hill
Then I went and stood upon some high old lonesome hill
Then looked down on the house where I used to live.

That's why the blues done called me to pack my things and go
That's why the blues done called me to pack my things and go
Cause my house fell down and I can't live there no more.

Mmm-mmm, I can't move no more
Mmm-mmm, I can't move no more
There ain't no place for a poor old girl to go.

— Bessie Smith

Blind Lemon Jefferson

Blind Lemon Jefferson was born in 1897 on a farm near Wortham, Texas, the youngest of eight children. He was born blind. In 1907 his only full brother, John, fell under a freight train and was cut to pieces. When he was 14 Blind Lemon began to play the guitar and sing. Begging on the streets with a guitar was one way for a poor, uneducated blind boy to make a living. Soon he became popular singing and playing for farm parties and dances. The country people thought that God had given Blind Lemon a gift in his fingers to make up for the blindness.

In 1917, when he was 20, he moved to Dallas to be on his own. But once he was away from home, he found it wasn't easy to make enough money for room and board. His weight of 250 pounds got him a job as a wrestler, and the novelty of a blind wrestler drew good crowds. When he began to make enough money to give himself a start, he quit wrestling and concentrated again on his music. With his friend Huddie "Leadbelly" Ledbetter he played in the streets and at dances. He sang in saloons and other night places. In a few years he was able to buy a car and hire a driver. In 1922 he was married.

Blind Lemon Jefferson

Blind Lemon learned from all kinds of songs and all styles of singers, and out of them developed his own style. He left Dallas and traveled around the South. He became well known. He began to spend his money on liquor and women. What he earned one day would be gone the next. His wife left him.

His first record came out in 1926. The songs were "Booster Blues" and "Dry Southern Blues." The record was successful, and he continued recording. Other songs he recorded were "Black Snake Moan," "Oil Well Blues," and "Tin Cup Blues." Altogether he made 80 records between 1926 and 1929. For each record he made, the company usually gave him a few dollars, a bottle, and a woman. He received very little in royalties from the records sold. In 1928 Blind Lemon began to lose his popularity. He wasn't as good on the city blues that were in demand. And many people disliked him because of his personal habits.

One night in Chicago, in February 1930, Blind Lemon left the recording studio to go to sing at a house party. The next morning his frozen body was found in the street, the guitar beside him. He was buried in a country graveyard in Texas. His grave is unmarked.

Blind Lemon Jefferson influenced many other blues singers who carried on the country blues tradition.

Leroy Carr

Leroy Carr

In the late 1920's and early 1930's the city blues were more popular than the country-style guitar blues. One of the men who brought about this change in style was a piano player named Leroy Carr.

Leroy was born in Nashville, Tennessee, in 1899, an only child. His father was a porter at Vanderbilt University in Nashville. In 1915 Leroy graduated from high school and went to work in a clothing store. In 1918 he began to learn the piano from men who played at local dance halls. In 1922 he started playing at the Gold Star Dance Hall, accompanying a singer. When the singer quit to become a baseball player, Leroy started singing himself. He became popular. Soon he was even able to buy clothes from the store where he had worked.

In 1928 he moved to Chicago to make records. He met guitarist Scrapper Blackwell, and they worked together. Their first record, "How Long How Long Blues," was a hit. By 1934 Leroy had recorded 100 blues. His style was simple and direct, with a quality of quiet sadness. More educated than other blues singers, he was able to approach the blues as a musical form.

After a while, Leroy and Scrapper weren't getting along so well. Scrapper accused Leroy of getting all the fame and money. The team broke up. Leroy made a few records alone, but they weren't very good.

Leroy died in Memphis in 1935. Some said he died of tuberculosis. Others said it was pneumonia. Others said he was poisoned.

A month after Leroy's death Scrapper Blackwell recorded "My Old Pal Blues."

Rabbit Brown

Rabbit Brown was a blues singer well known in New Orleans around the time of World War I. He was born in New Orleans and lived there until his death in 1937.

Rabbit was from the James Alley neighborhood, a narrow street behind the city jail. It was called "the battleground" because of the gang fights that took place there. Children played ball in the alley, and old men peddled candy or vegetables. Louis Armstrong was born and raised in James Alley.

As a young man Rabbit began to make his living playing the guitar and singing in the night places. He entertained the employees and customers with songs like "If They Could See You Back at the Plantation What Would They Think of You Now?" He was popular in New Orleans because he could make up on-the-spot songs about local people. He listened to street singers from the country and learned the country-style blues from them. In 1917 the night places were closed down, and hard times came to Rabbit. He became a bitter man.

The one record that brought him fame was made right there in the streets of New Orleans. It was "James Alley Blues."

Rabbit Brown died in New Orleans in 1937, poor and lonely.

Jane Alley in New Orleans, 1958. Known as "James Alley," this neighborhood was the birthplace of Louis Armstrong and Rabbit Brown. The buildings of Jane Alley have been torn down to make room for a modern steel and concrete addition to the police station.

Leadbelly

Leadbelly

During his lifetime Huddie "Leadbelly" Ledbetter, composer of such well-known songs as "Goodnight Irene" and "Take This Hammer," met with discouragement and frustration. He had to die before he was accepted.

Leadbelly was born in Mooringsport, in the backwoods part of Louisiana, around 1885. During his early years he wandered around Texas, northern Louisiana, and parts of Arkansas and Oklahoma. He heard all kinds of music, especially rural music, and put what he learned into his own songs. He associated with people of many different backgrounds, and developed a rich variety in his music. Although his work on the 12-string guitar was widely copied, the title "King of the 12-string Guitar" still belongs to Leadbelly. From the French Cajuns of northern Louisiana, he learned to play the windjammer, a kind of accordian, which he played at country dances. He also played the mandolin, string bass, and piano. For a while he traveled with Blind Lemon Jefferson and picked up some of his style.

In 1918 Leadbelly was convicted of murder and sent to the Shaw State Prison Farm in Texas. In prison he learned the art of playing the fool in order to get along with white men. Pat Neff, the governor of Texas, who was interested in folklore, knew that some of the best American music was being sung right there in the prison. For the governor, Leadbelly sang his "Freedom Song," in which he appealed for a pardon. The governor did not grant the pardon, but after his term as governor had ended, he helped get Leadbelly released in 1925.

On February 28, 1930, Leadbelly was sentenced to 10 years in Angola Penitentiary in Louisiana for assault with intent to murder. He had gotten into a fight over some whiskey two men had tried to take from his dinner pail. Angola Penitentiary was tough. In 1931 Leadbelly received 10 lashes for laziness. In 1932 he received 15 lashes for impudence. At Angola he was discovered by John A. Lomax, who was traveling about the South recording "authentic" folk music for the Library of Congress. He was released from the penitentiary in 1934 because of "good time" he had earned in prison.

In 1935 he married Martha Promise and took a job as John Lomax's chauffeur. He went to New York and continued recording for John and Alan Lomax until 1942. Leadbelly had a hard time in New York. In 1939-40 he served a year in prison for third degree assault. He broke off with the Lomaxes because he felt they were exploiting him. He couldn't find an identity in his new life. Folk music was not in demand then. A country Negro singer like Leadbelly was a strange curiosity to white city audiences. Other Negro performers sang and played for Negro audiences, on Negro radio stations, and in Negro clubs. Their records were made for the race market. Leadbelly had been drawn into the white entertainment world, and the white world didn't know what to make of him. They couldn't accept him for what he was, and he kept searching for an image that they could accept. Younger Negroes disliked him because he was southern and country. Older blacks locked him out because he associated with white people and sang for white audiences. In those days there were no coffee houses, no folk concerts, no long-playing record albums, no big guitar sales. Leadbelly was a lonely pioneer, breaking new ground from which others would reap a harvest.

There were a few friends, such as folk musicians Woody Guthrie and Pete Seeger. Pete especially was a fan of Leadbelly and presented much of his music to the public. Leadbelly appeared occasionally at the Village Vanguard in New York. He played for rallies, parties, children in public squares, for anyone who would listen to him. And among these audiences he planted the seeds of the folk music revival that blossomed 10 years after his death.

Leadbelly died poor at Bellevue Hospital in New York on December 14, 1949. In 1950 "Goodnight Irene" swept the country.

Blind Willie Johnson

Willie Johnson was born on a farm near Marlin, Texas, in 1902. In 1905 his mother died and his father remarried. When he was 7 his father caught his stepmother with another man and beat her. To get even, she threw a pan of lye water in Willie's face and blinded him.

As a boy Blind Willie began to beg in the streets as a street singer. Even then there was sadness and loneliness in his music. He continued playing in the streets of Marlin and began singing in churches and at religious meetings. He kept a tin cup fastened to the neck of his guitar. When his father went shopping in the city, he would bring Willie with him, and Willie would sing while his father shopped.

In Dallas in 1927 he met a girl named Angeline. She saw him singing a hymn in the street and invited him to her house to sing hymns. They sang, he ate, and he proposed. They were married the next day and settled in Beaumont, Texas.

BLIND WILLIE JOHNSON

This new and exclusive Columbia artist, Blind Willie Johnson, sings sacred selections in a way that you have never heard before. Be sure to hear his first record and listen close to that guitar accompaniment. Nothing like it anywhere else.

Record No. 14276-D, 10-Inch, 75c

I Know His Blood Can Make Me Whole

Jesus Make Up My Dying Bed

Ask Your Dealer for Latest Race Record Catalog

Columbia Phonograph Company, 1819 Broadway, New York City

Columbia
NEW PROCESS RECORDS
Made the New Way - Electrically

Advertisement for Blind Willie Johnson's first record, 1927.

In December 1927 he began his recording career. His songs express deep feelings of pain and grief: "Motherless Children Have a Hard Time," "Dark Was the Night and Cold the Ground," "I Know His Blood Can Make Me Whole." His songs were popular during the depression of the 1930's because they combined grief and pain with a turning to God for help. Willie was one of the best country guitarists. He used his voice like a musical instrument playing a duet with his guitar. Sometimes he slid a pocket knife along the strings Hawaiian style.

At the end of the depression Willie quit recording. He stayed in Beaumont, where he is remembered as a gentle, dignified man. In the late 1940's a jazz and gospel music revival brought him new fame, but Willie continued living a poor life in Beaumont. In 1949 his house burned. He and Angeline spent the night in the ruins of the house, sleeping on water-soaked mattresses. The next day Willie went out to earn some money singing in the streets. He caught pneumonia and died.

Big Bill Broonzy

"They tell me I'm singin' 'folk songs.' I suppose they must be right. I guess my songs is folks' songs. I ain't never heard a horse sing." Those are the words of William Lee Conley Broonzy, commonly known as Big Bill.

Big Bill Broonzy was born in Scott, Mississippi, in either 1893 or 1898, depending on whether you believe Bill or his twin sister. He was one of 17 children. His grandmother was a mulatto. When she married his grandfather, her family threw her out of the house for marrying a black man. When Bill walked his grandmother to church, he had to wait outside because he was too black to be allowed in the church. His father and mother were slaves when they met. She would be whipped for not getting her quota of cotton picked. He, feeling sorry for her, would finish his work quick and help her. After they were freed they got married. When Bill was still a small child, the family moved to Arkansas.

When he was 10, Bill made a cigar box fiddle. Then someone bought him a real fiddle and he learned to play it. He started out wanting to be a preacher, but when he found he could make more money fiddling at picnics and dances, he changed his mind about preaching. Eventually he moved on from the fiddle to the guitar. Bill served in the U.S. Army during World War I. After the war, because he couldn't stand to live in Arkansas any more, he went north. In 1920 he got a job as a redcap in Chicago. His first record, made around 1925, was "House Rent Stomp" and "Big Bill Blues." He received no money for the recording. The record company misspelled his name on the record, calling him "Big Bill Broomsley."

Big Bill did not grow up with the country blues tradition. He learned by imitation, eventually developing his own warm, personal style. Between 1934 and 1937 he recorded with a piano player, Black Bob. One of their most popular records was "Take Your Hands Off Her." He became a successful pop blues singer, very popular with black audiences in the 1930's and 1940's. In the 1950's Big Bill was introduced as an ex-sharecropper and labeled a "folk artist" for the benefit of young white folk music fans who didn't know him from the old days. He returned to the country blues, which were having a revival.

He got a job as janitor at Iowa State College, and would go to Chicago periodically to record. During the fifties he made concert tours of France and England and was very popular in those countries. He wrote his life story, *Big Bill's Blues,* in which he tells about his songs and the stories behind them. In one song, "Black, Brown, and White," he expresses his feelings about discrimination. He says that if you're white, you'll be all right, if you're

Big Bill Broonzy
receives flowers
after performance.

brown, you can stick around, but if you're black, brother,
you have to git back, git back, git back. The song was un-
popular with Negroes because it criticized lighter Negroes
who discriminated against the darker country Negroes
from the South, instead of helping them.

In the late fifties Bill developed cancer of the throat,
and an operation took away his voice. He died in Chicago
in August 1959.

Black, Brown, and White

This little song that I'm singing about
People you know is true
If you're black and got to work for a living
This is what they will say to you

Refrain: They say if you's white, you's all right
             If you's brown, stick around
             But as you're black
             Mmm, Mmm, Brother, git back, git back, git back

I was in a place one night
They was all having fun
They was all buying beer and wine
But they would not sell me none

Refrain

Me and a man was working side by side
This is what it meant
They was paying him a dollar an hour
And they was paying me fifty cents

Refrain

I went to an employment office
Got a number and got in line
They called everybody's number
But they never did call mine

Refrain

I helped win sweet victory
With my little plow and hoe
Now I want you to tell me, brother
What you gonna do about old Jim Crow

Refrain

I helped build the country
And I fought for it too
Now I guess you can see
What a black man has to do

Refrain

— Big Bill Broonzy

"Black, Brown and White" by Big Bill Broonzy
© Cassell and Company Ltd., London
from BIG BILL BLUES: William Broonzy's Story
as told to Yannick Bruyhoghe
© 1955, 1964 Oak Publications, Inc., New York
Used by Permission

Billie Holiday

Billie Holiday was born Eleanora Fagan Gough, on April 7, 1915, in Baltimore, Maryland. Three years later her parents married. Her father, Clarence Holiday, played trumpet, banjo, and guitar, and was often on the road. When Eleanora, who later took the name Billie after movie actress Billie Dove, was still very young, her parents separated. Her mother left her with relatives and went to New York to look for work.

Billie had some rough experiences in her childhood. Once she lay down to rest with her great-grandmother, whom she loved very much. She woke up hours later with her dead great-grandmother's stiff, cold arm around her neck. Billie spent a month in the hospital recovering from the shock. To make matters worse a cousin who disliked her continued to make her feel guilty about the old woman's death. When she was 10 she was attacked by a man in the neighborhood. After this incident Billie was sent to a Catholic Home for Girls. The lonely, unhappy girl learned early in life how to scrap and stand up for herself.

In 1928 she went to New York to join her mother. She decided to visit Harlem first, and got lost. A social worker put her up in what Billie thought was a beautiful hotel until her mother could be located. Years later, as an adult, Billie went out of curiosity to look up this hotel. It was the YWCA.

At 14 she smoked her first reefer. She worked as an errand girl for the proprietress of a night place. It was here that she first listened to records of Bessie Smith, Louis Armstrong, and other jazz musicians. At 15 she served a jail term for walking the streets of Harlem.

During the depression Billie went to a speakeasy in Harlem and asked for a job as a dancer. She danced for the owner, who reacted by telling her she was lousy. Then she sang "Trav'lin' All Alone." All the customers stopped to look and listen. Billie was hired at $18 a week, and it wasn't long before well-known musicians were coming to hear her sing. In 1933 she began to make records. Her first records were poor, but later ones were hits. Billie's voice had a sour-sweet quality. She sang with controlled emotion. She was a beautiful, warm, friendly person who never let her success go to her head. People nicknamed her "Lady Day." Her most memorable song was "Strange

Billie Holiday in the film *New Orleans*

Fruit," written by Lewis Allan, which describes the black bodies of lynched Negroes hanging from the poplar trees.

In 1938 Billie Holiday broke the color bar when she joined Artie Shaw's band. For a black singer to perform with a white orchestra was an outstanding achievement, and it had its price. When Billie traveled with the band, she often experienced bitter discrimination. At one restaurant everyone was waited on except Billie. She was served only when the other band members ordered the waitress to do it. At some places she was not permitted to use the bathroom. Sometimes, instead of sitting on the bandstand with the orchestra, as other singers did, she had to wait in a little room by herself, and come out just long enough to do her number. At times the tough little girl from the streets could not resist fighting back. Once she threw a glass at a man who called her "nigger." At one night club she stuck a woman's head in a toilet bowl for calling her a dirty name.

In the early 1940's she appeared in a movie, *New Orleans*. She played a maid, the only type of role available to a black, but it gave her a chance to sing on the screen. By this time Billie was considered the top singer in the country.

Then the downhill road began. Billie got hooked on heroin. She tried private hospital cures but failed. She volunteered to go to a federal rehabilitation hospital, where she endured the "cold turkey" treatment. While there she washed dishes, peeled potatoes, and fed pigs. When she returned to New York she played to a full house at a concert in Carnegie Hall. But the problem continued. Her singing now had a bitter, painful quality. She felt that her problem was made harder by our laws that treat addicts as criminals rather than sick people. She was hounded by both the police and the dope-pushers. In New York she was refused a performer's license to work in cabarets. Some of her old friends turned their backs on her.

Money from royalties that had piled up while she was at the hospital was squandered by parasite managers and agents. In 1949 she was framed by a manager who handed her a package of opium just before a police raid. She stood trial and was found not guilty. A priest and a psychiatrist helped her to overcome the desire to die.

In 1954 and 1958 Billie toured Europe and was successful. She seemed to be getting back her old style, but no other singer put so much feeling into the words "hunger" and "love." And her old problems continued to haunt her. Thin, pale, and coughing, she made her last public appearance at the Phoenix Theatre in New York in June 1959. A week later she was taken to the hospital, where the police arrested her on her deathbed. On June 17, 1959, she escaped them. Lady Day was dead.

Strange Fruit

Southern trees bear a strange fruit,
Blood on the leaves and blood at the root,
Black body swinging in the Southern breeze,
Strange fruit hanging from the poplar trees.

Pastoral scene of the gallant South,
The bulging eyes and the twisted mouth,
Scent of magnolia sweet and fresh,
And the sudden smell of burning flesh!

Here is a fruit for the crows to pluck,
For the rain to gather, for the wind to suck,
For the sun to rot, for a tree to drop,
Here is a strange and bitter crop.

—Lewis Allan

"Strange Fruit" by Lewis Allan
© Edward B. Marks Music Corporation
Used by Permission

Billie Holiday

Lonnie Johnson

Lonnie Johnson, blues singer and jazz guitarist, was born February 2, 1889, in New Orleans. He was one of 11 children in the family. In 1915 all the children except Lonnie and James died of influenza. As a child Lonnie studied guitar and violin, and eventually learned the piano and the kazoo. During World War I Lonnie and James played in New Orleans theatres. From 1917 to 1919 they appeared in a revue in London.

After the war Lonnie joined a band on the river steamer *St. Paul,* but in 1922 he had an argument with the band leader and left the group. For a few years his music career was at a standstill. He took a job in a tire factory in Galesburg, Illinois. In 1925 he moved to East St. Louis, Illinois, got a job in a steel foundry, and got married.

He started moving in music again when he won a blues contest at the Booker T. Washington Theatre in St. Louis. Then he cut his first record, "Mr. Johnson's Blues" and "Falling Rain Blues." He learned the country blues style. He played in theatres and recorded in Chicago and New York. His recording of "Mean Old Bed Bug Blues" was a big hit, and there was a big demand for his music. He was very popular during the 1920's and is considered the best jazz guitarist of that period. He recorded with Louis Armstrong and Duke Ellington. Some of his best songs, "These Blues Like Me," "I Just Can't Stand the Blues," and "Careless Love," did not sell well because the public preferred songs that were cheap and dirty.

Lonnie Johnson

From 1932 to 1937 there was a lull in Lonnie's career. He spent those years in Cleveland doing some radio work and other jobs. In 1937 he started recording again. Around 1945 he took up the amplified guitar and switched from blues to ballads. In 1952 he toured England. Then there were more lean years. His music didn't appeal to audiences of the 1950's. In 1958 he was seen by an old friend, sick and shabby. Between 1958 and 1960 he worked as a chef in a Philadelphia hotel. Then he began to make public appearances again. In 1961 he appeared at Gerdes Folk City in New York with Victoria Spivey, with whom he had made some records almost 35 years earlier. In 1964 he toured England again. Six years later, Lonnie Johnson died in Toronto, Canada.

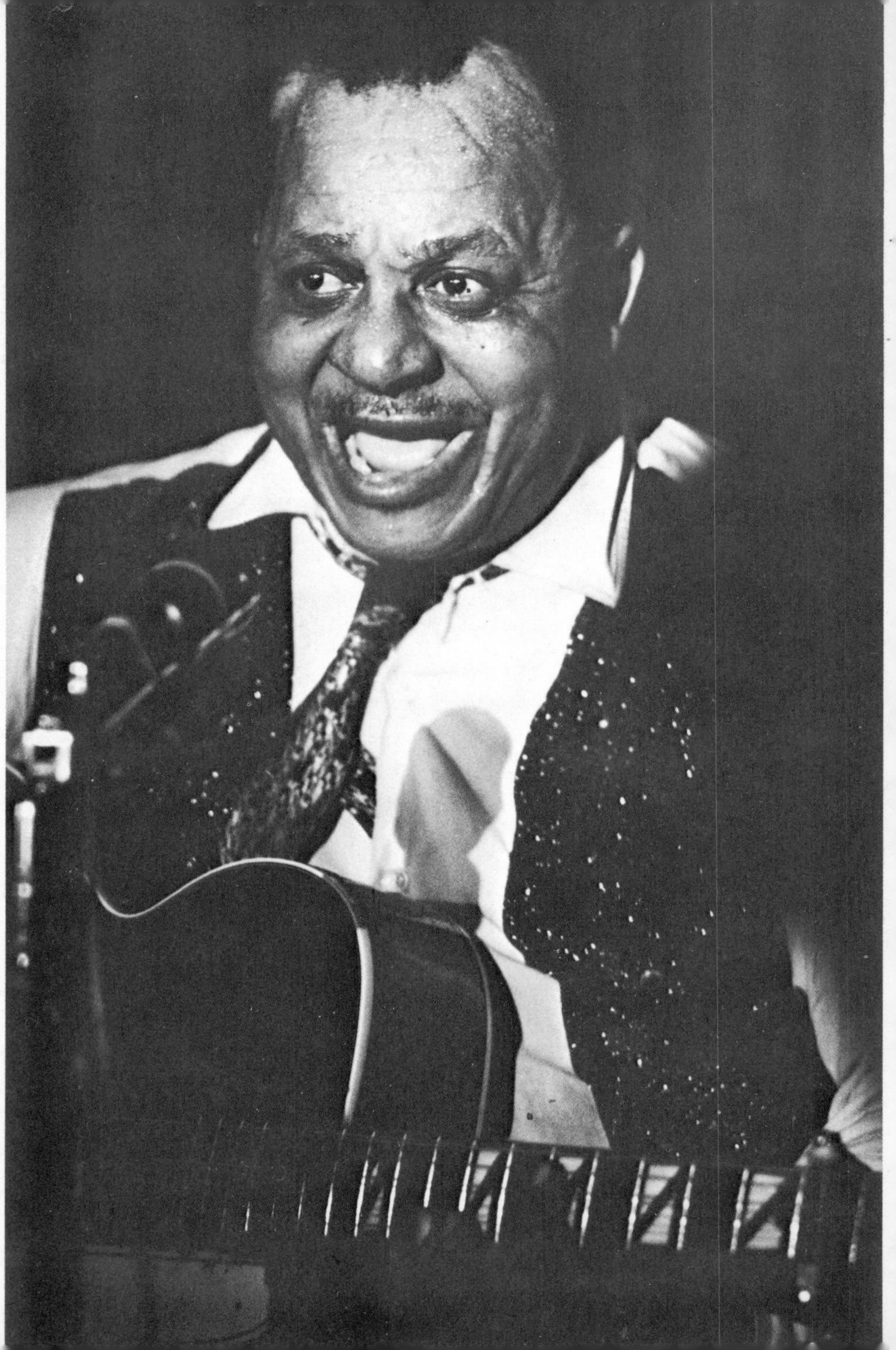

Big Joe Williams

Big Joe Williams, sometimes known as Poor Joe, was born around 1900 in Crawford, Mississippi. He was one of 16 children. As a boy he made himself a guitar out of a cigar box. At 15 he got a real guitar and started making up blues.

Joe left home and went to work in levee camps along the Mississippi and on railroad gangs. The levee work was hard. The camps were just a bunch of tents or shacks. The pay was $1.50 a day for a 12-to-16-hour day. The railroad was a little better, because the men lived in boxcars and were able to get into town. Life as a wandering worker made Big Joe tough.

He began to play for dances and picnics. He added strings to his guitar and eventually settled on one with nine strings. He joined a medicine show with a jug band. In 1930 he went to Chicago and made some records, including "Whoopee Blues," "Tell Me Baby," and "The Dead Gone Train." During the depression he worked for the WPA on levee gangs. After the depression he began recording again. In the 1950's he was recording for a small company in St. Louis.

In 1963 Big Joe played at a concert in Chicago. His guitar work was described as crude and stinging, his

singing style harsh and primitive. Among his numbers were "Mink Coat Blues" and "Sloppy Drunk Blues." He made a European tour, but it earned him little money, most of which he had to spend on dental work.

In 1964 Big Joe was sleeping on a folding cot in the basement of a record shop, acting as night watchman in exchange for a place to sleep. The blues revival had brought him some new fame, but not much money.

Tommy McClennan

Tommy McClennan was born April 8, 1908, on a farm nine miles out of Yazoo City, Mississippi. As a boy he worked on the farm and on weekends went into town to entertain himself in barrooms, theatres, or poolrooms. He began playing the guitar when he was in his teens. He began recording in Jackson, Mississippi, and then moved to Chicago to continue his recording career.

Tommy was a small, thin man. He was a nervous man and a heavy drinker. His singing style was harsh and fierce, with moments of shouting and laughter. His songs were often boastful. Among his better known songs were "Bottle It Up and Go," "Whiskey Head Woman," and "Whiskey Head Man."

Once in Chicago he went to a party with his friend Big Bill Broonzy. Big Bill warned Tommy that, though southern Negroes referred to themselves as "nigger," northern Negroes didn't like the word. Tommy ignored Bill's warning and sang a song with the word "nigger." It started a fight, and Tommy had to get away by jumping out the window.

Tommy was dropped by the record company because he was drinking too much. He died in the late 1950's, a drifter in Chicago's Skid Row.

Furry Lewis

Walter Lewis was born March 3, 1893, in Greenwood, Mississippi. When he was six his family moved to Memphis. His school friends nicknamed him Furry. In 1917 Furry lost a leg in a railroad accident. He learned to sing and play the guitar to make a living, and got his start traveling around with medicine shows.

Furry invented the "Mississippi Bottle Neck" method of guitar-playing. He broke the neck off a bottle and heated it in fire so that the broken edge would melt smooth. Then he put it on the little finger of his left hand and slid it along the strings to play a melody. He played in a jug band, and he and Jim Jackson, another member of the band, scored a hit with "Goin' to Kansas City."

In 1927 Furry recorded in Chicago. Then he returned to Memphis and went to work in a garage, but also recorded several songs in Memphis. Furry's style was to talk his songs to elaborate guitar playing.

Furry's hands

During the 1950's, Furry worked for the city of Memphis as a street cleaner. People wouldn't even believe him when he told them that he was once a successful recording star. But in later years, Furry began making records and personal appearances again. He was honored as a great blues performer. On his 80th birthday, Furry talked about his life and his music. "The good Lord has been good to me," he said. "I guess, mighty good."

Furry Lewis

Lightnin' Hopkins

Sam "Lightnin'" Hopkins is known in Houston, Texas, as the city's leading street singer. He is known throughout the world as one of the last and greatest of the traditional country blues singers.

Sam Hopkins was born March 15, 1912, in Centerville, Texas. As a boy he sang in church to please his mother, and there, just by fooling around, he learned to play the organ and piano. He learned the guitar from his cousin, Texas Alexander, and from Blind Lemon Jefferson. When he was nine, he left home with his guitar slung across his shoulder. He worked on a farm near Centerville, and later composed a blues song about his life there, "Tim Moore's Farm." As he grew older, he lived off what he made from gambling and singing. He stayed away from people who called him "Boy" and expected him to say "Yessuh."

In his early music career he worked with Texas Alexander and a piano player named Thunder Smith. In 1946 he and Thunder recorded in Hollywood as Thunder Smith and Lightnin' Hopkins. The name stayed with him.

A year later he returned to Houston and made some records for a small company. He was a hit. He went to New York and did some recording there. Lightnin' worked alone, using just his voice, his unamplified guitar, and his talent. He went back to the early work songs and field songs for his basic material, and improvised on it as he sang. This improvising sometimes made things difficult for those recording him, because no two takes of the same song were ever alike. He continued recording in New York

Lightnin'
Hopkins

in the 1950's and then went back to live in Houston. For a few years he lived away from the limelight, singing for his friends and neighbors in Houston. Then he was rediscovered, and in the 1960's, using Houston as his home base, began recording again and making concert appearances. He has appeared in concerts in Chicago and New York, and in 1964 made a concert tour of England.

Lightnin' still likes his own private world of Houston's sidewalks. He is not tempted by fame. He is suspicious of the outside world—especially the commercial world—that he feels would like to cast him into a mold. Lightnin' is independent. He sings his own songs in his own way. His style is direct. His voice can be raw and harsh or soft and sensitive. His material is sad or humorous. He sings about poverty, gambling, bad men, hard work, and escape; about current happenings, bus strikes, and his personal experiences. One of his most popular songs is "Short-Haired Woman," about a woman's attempts to have her hair straightened. He is always individual and personal. He never cheapens his material to please his audiences, but sings "like he is." Record companies have learned to let him be himself when he records, allowing him to improvise and follow his own direction without hindering him.

Some people consider Lightnin' one of a dying breed. The younger blacks think he is old-fashioned. The younger whites seem to like his protest songs better than his personal blues. But Lightnin' feels that when the rock-and-roll groups are gone and forgotten he'll still be wailin' the blues.

Muddy Waters

McKinley Morganfield, known today as Muddy Waters, was born April 14, 1915, in Rolling Fork, Mississippi. His mother died when he was three, and he was raised in Clarksdale, Mississippi, by his grandmother. As a young man, when he wasn't working in the cotton fields, he began to learn the guitar. Folklorist Alan Lomax discovered him singing in the cotton fields and recorded him for the Library of Congress. For this recording he sang "I Be's Troubled" and "Country Blues."

He stayed on the farm one more year, gaining experience by playing at dances and parties. He learned the harmonica and joined a traveling tent show as a harmonica accompanist. In 1943 he went to Chicago. He worked in a paper mill and as a truck driver. Then he met Big Bill Broonzy and other Chicago blues singers and began to learn their style. He switched from country blues to Chicago blues. He got an electric guitar and started recording. He organized his own group, consisting of a piano, two guitars, a harmonica, a bass, and drums. He has gone in for electrified, amplified music, the loud urban sound. One of his biggest hits is "Hoochie Coochie Man," a song about love charms.

Muddy Waters

Sonny Terry

Sonny Terry

Saunders Teddell, now known as Sonny Terry, blues singer and harmonica player, was born October 24, 1911, in Durham, North Carolina. His father, Reuben Teddell, was a farmer. When Sonny was 11, he was beating a stick against a chair, and a piece of it flew off and injured his eye. Five years later a boy threw a small piece of iron at him and put out the other eye. He learned the harmonica and juice harp from his father. In 1924 his father bought a phonograph, and Sonny was able to hear Ma Rainey, Blind Lemon, and other blues singers.

He went into Durham and Raleigh to play in the streets. When he was 23 he met guitarist Blind Boy Fuller. They became close friends, singing and playing together in the streets. In 1937 Fuller recorded in New York, and the next year Sonny joined him. They recorded almost 20 blues together. In 1938 Sonny appeared in a concert at Carnegie Hall. A young man from the country, standing alone in the middle of the stage with his harmonica, he took the audience by storm. He made a few records with a washboard player named Oh Red, including "Harmonica Stomp" and "Harmonica and Washboard Blues."

In the early 1940's he teamed with guitarist Brownie McGhee, and they have worked together since then, living within a few blocks of each other in New York. In 1946-47 he appeared in the Broadway musical *Finian's Rainbow,* and from 1955 to 1957 he appeared in Tennessee Williams' play, *Cat on a Hot Tin Roof.* He and Brownie have toured the United States, Europe, and even India.

Brownie McGhee

Walter Brown McGhee was born November 30, 1915, in Knoxville, Tennessee, one of four children. When he was four he was stricken with polio, which made his right leg shorter than his left. Brownie's father was a country singer and guitar player, and his uncle played the fiddle. Brownie learned music on an instrument his uncle made for him, a 5-string banjo with a marshmallow can for the head and a neck made of poplar wood. When the family moved to Lenoir City, Tennessee, Brownie began to play the church organ and sang in a church quartet. When the family moved to Maryville, he began to entertain in resorts in the Smokey Mountains, playing the guitar and kazoo.

He quit high school and hitch-hiked around the state with his guitar. He watched blues singers perform. He traveled with carnivals and medicine shows. He returned home and worked with his father in a gospel quartet. He began playing with bands at picnics and dances.

In 1938 Brownie went into North Carolina and did some street singing. From there he went to Chicago to make some recordings, including "Step It Up and Go" and "Workingman's Blues." He began working with Sonny Terry in New York, performing in folk song concerts,

Brownie McGhee

night clubs, and the streets. After World War II he started Brownie McGhee's School of the Blues, giving lessons to young singers and guitarists. He recorded one of his most popular songs, "Sporting Life Blues." He appeared in the Broadway shows *Cat on a Hot Tin Roof* and *Simply Heavenly*.

He and Sonny have continued performing and recording together, and remain very popular. Brownie is married and lives in New York.

The Pull Ahead Books

AMERICA'S FIRST LADIES
  1789 to 1865

AMERICA'S FIRST LADIES
  1865 to the Present Day

DARING SEA CAPTAINS

DOERS AND DREAMERS

FAMOUS CHESS PLAYERS

FAMOUS CRIMEFIGHTERS

FAMOUS SPIES

GREAT AMERICAN NATURALISTS

INDIAN CHIEFS

PIRATES AND BUCCANEERS

POLITICAL CARTOONISTS

PRESIDENTIAL LOSERS

SINGERS OF THE BLUES

STARS OF THE ZIEGFELD FOLLIES

WESTERN LAWMEN

WESTERN OUTLAWS

We specialize in publishing quality books for young people. For a complete list please write

LERNER PUBLICATIONS COMPANY

241 First Avenue North, Minneapolis, Minnesota 55401

727920

784.0922

Surge, Frank.
    Singers of the blues. Minneapolis,
Lerner Publications Co. [1969]
    63 p. illus., ports. 21 cm. (A Pull
ahead book)
    SUMMARY: Brief biographies of
seventeen singers and musicians who
helped develop the blues style and
became legendary performers during
their lifetime.

    1. Singers, American--Biography.
2. Jazz musicians--Biography.   3. Afro-
American musicians--Biography.
    I. Title